Born in 1932

by

Kerry Butters.

Born in 1932.

Millennium: 2nd millennium

Centuries: 19th century – **20th century** – 21st century

Decades: 1900s 1910s 1920s – **1930s** – 1940s 1950s 1960s

Years: 1929 1930 1931 – **1932** – 1933 1934 1935

1932 (MCMXXXII) was a leap year starting on Friday (dominical letter CB) of the Gregorian calendar, the 1932nd year of the Common Era (CE) and *Anno Domini* (AD) designations, the 932nd year of the 2nd millennium, the 32nd year of the 20th century, and the 3rd year of the 1930s decade.

Contents

Events

January

- January 1 – The United States Post Office Department issues a set of 12 stamps commemorating the 200th anniversary of George Washington's birth.
- January 3 – The British arrest and intern Mohandas Gandhi and Vallabhbhai Patel.
- January 7 – The Stimson Doctrine is proclaimed, in response to the Japanese invasion of Manchuria.
- January 8 – In Great Britain the Archbishop of Canterbury forbids Anglican church remarriage of divorced persons.
- January 9 – Sakuradamon Incident, Korean nationalist Lee Bong-chang fails in his effort to assassinate Hirohito Emperor of Japan. The Kuomintang's official newspaper runs an editorial expressing regret that the attempt failed, which is used by the Japanese as a pretext to attack Shanghai later in the month.
- January 12 – Hattie W. Caraway becomes the first woman elected to the United States Senate.
- January 14 – Maurice Ravel's Concerto in G debuts with piano soloist Marguerite Long and Ravel conducting the Lamoureux Orchestra.
- January 15 – About 6 million are unemployed in Germany.
- January 22 – The 1932 Salvadoran peasant uprising begins, it is suppressed by the government of Maximiliano Hernández Martínez

- January 24 – Marshal Pietro Badoglio declares the end of Libyan resistance.
- January 26 – The British submarine *M2* sinks with all 60 hands.
- January 28 – Conflict between Japan and China in the Battle of Shanghai.
- January 29 – The minority government of Karl Buresch in Austria ends the governmental crisis.
- January 31 – Japanese warships arrive in Nanking.

February

- February 1 – *Brave New World*, a novel by Aldous Huxley, is first published.
- February 2
  - A general World Disarmament Conference begins in Geneva. The principal issue at the conference is the demand made by Germany for *gleichberechtigung* ("equality of status" i.e. abolishing Part V of the Treaty of Versailles, which had disarmed Germany) and the French demand for *sécurité* ("security" i.e. maintaining Part V).
  - The League of Nations again recommends negotiations between the Republic of China and Japan.
  - The Reconstruction Finance Corporation begins operations in Washington, D.C.
- February 4
  - The 1932 Winter Olympics open in Lake Placid, New York.
  - Japan occupies Harbin, China.
- February 9 – Junnosuke Inoue, prominent Japanese businessman, banker and former governor of the Bank of Japan is assassinated by right-wing extremist group the League of Blood in the League of Blood Incident.
- February 11 – Pope Pius XI meets Benito Mussolini in Vatican City.
- February 15 – *Clara, Lu & Em*, generally regarded as the first daytime network soap opera, debuts in its morning time slot over

the Blue Network of NBC Radio, having originally been a late evening program.

- February 18 – Japan declares Manchukuo (Japanese name for Manchuria) formally independent from China.
- February 22 – The first Purple Heart is awarded.
- February 24 – Women's suffrage is granted in Brazil.
- February 25 – Adolf Hitler obtains German citizenship by naturalization, opening the opportunity for him to run in the 1932 election for Reichspräsident.
- February 27 – The Mäntsälä rebellion occurs in Finland.

March

- March 1
  o Charles Lindbergh, Jr., the infant son of Anne Morrow Lindbergh and Charles Lindbergh, is kidnapped from the family home near Hopewell, New Jersey.
  o Japan proclaims Manchuria an independent state and installs Puyi as puppet emperor.
- March 2 – The Mäntsälä rebellion ends in failure; Finnish democracy prevails. The Lapua Movement is condemned by conservative Finnish President Pehr Evind Svinhufvud in a radio speech.
- March 5 – Dan Takuma, prominent Japanese businessman and director of the Mitsui *Zaibatsu* conglomerate is assassinated by the radical right-wing League of Blood group.
- March 7 – Four people are killed when police fire upon 3,000 unemployed autoworkers marching outside the Ford River Rouge Plant in Dearborn, Michigan.
- March 9 – Éamon de Valera is elected President of the Executive Council of the Irish Free State. It is the first change of government in the Irish Free State since its foundation 10 years previously.
- March 14 – George Eastman, founder of Kodak, commits suicide.
- March 18 – Peace negotiations between China and Japan begin.
- March 19 – The Sydney Harbour Bridge opens.

- March 20 – The *Graf Zeppelin* begins a regular route to South America.
- March 21– A series of deadly tornadoes in the south kills more than 220 people in Alabama, 34 in Georgia and 17 in Tennessee during a two-day period.
- March 25 – *Tarzan the Ape Man* opens, with Olympic gold medal swimmer Johnny Weissmuller in the title role. (Weismuller will star in a total of twelve *Tarzan* films.)

April

- April 5
  - 10,000 disgruntled Newfoundlanders march on their legislature to show discontent with their current political situation; this is a flash point in the demise of the Dominion of Newfoundland.
  - *Kreuger & Toll*, the company of the "Match King" Ivar Kreuger, collapses.
  - The first Alko stores are opened in Finland at 10 in the morning (local time) following the end of Prohibition in that country, resulting in a new mnemonic "543210".
- April 6
  - U.S. president Herbert Hoover supports armament limitations at the World Disarmament Conference.
  - The trial against fraudulent art dealer Otto Wacker begins in Berlin.
- April 11 – Paul von Hindenburg is re-elected president of Germany.
- April 13 – German Chancellor Heinrich Brüning bans the SA and the SS as threats to public order, arguing that they are chiefly responsible for the wave of political violence afflicting Germany.
- April 14 – John Cockcroft and Ernest Walton focus a proton beam on lithium and split its nucleus.
- April 17 – Haile Selassie announces an anti-slavery law in Abyssinia.

- April 19 – German art dealer Otto Wacker is sentenced to 19 months in prison for selling fraudulent paintings he attributed to Vincent van Gogh.
- April 25 – Two of the companions of Islamic prophet Muhammad are moved from their graves upon informing of water in the graves in the dream of King Faisal of Iraq in Salmaan Paak, Iraq. Their names are Hudhayfah ibn al-Yaman and Jabir ibn Abd Allah.
- April 29 – Korean pro-independence paramilitary Yun Bong-gil detonates a bomb at a gathering of Japanese government and mililtary officials in Shanghai's Hongkou Park, killing General Yoshinori Shirakawa and injuring Mamoru Shigemitsu and Vice Admiral Kichisaburō Nomura.

May

- May 2 – Comedian Jack Benny's radio show airs for the first time.
- May 6 – Paul Gorguloff shoots French president Paul Doumer in Paris; Doumer dies the next day.
- May 6 – The politically powerful General Kurt von Schleicher meets secretly with Adolf Hitler. General Schleicher tells Hitler that he is scheming to bring down the Brüning government and asks for Nazi support of the new "presidential government" Schleicher is planning to form. Schleicher and Hitler negotiated a "gentlemen's agreement" where in exchange for lifting the ban on the SA and SS and having the *Reichstag* dissolved for early elections that summer, the Nazis will support Schleicher's new chancellor.
- May 10 –
  - Albert Lebrun becomes the new president of France.
  - Violent scenes in the *Reichstag* as Hermann Göring and other Nazi MRDs attack the Defense Minister General Wilhelm Groener for his lack of belief in a supposed Social Democratic *putsch*. After the debate, General Schleicher tells Groener that he has lost the confidence of the Army and must resign at once.
  -

- May 12 –
  - Ten weeks after his abduction, the infant son of Charles Lindbergh is found dead just a few miles from the Lindbergh home.
  - General Wilhelm Groener resigns as Defense Minister. Schleicher takes control of the Defense Ministry.
- May 13 – The Premier of New South Wales, Jack Lang, is dismissed by the State Governor, Sir Philip Game.
- May 15 – Japanese troops leave Shanghai. Back in Japan, the May 15 Incident as an attempted military coup is known occurs. The Japanese prime minister Tsuyoshi Inukai is assassinated by naval officers.
- May 16 – Massive riots between Hindus and Muslims in Bombay leave thousands dead and injured.
- May 20–May 21 – Amelia Earhart flies from the United States to County Londonderry, Northern Ireland in 14 hours 54 minutes.
- May 20 – *Federación Obrera de la Industria de la Carne* initiates a major strike in the Argentinian meat-packing industry.
- May 26 – Judgement in Donoghue v Stevenson handed down in the House of Lords, creating the neighbour principle in English law.
- May 29 – The first of approximately 15,000 World War I veterans arrive in Washington, D.C. demanding the immediate payment of their military bonus, becoming known as the Bonus Army.
- May 30 – German chancellor Heinrich Brüning is dismissed by President von Hindenburg. President Hindenburg asks Franz von Papen to form a new government, known as the "Government of the President's Friends", which is openly dedicated to the destruction of democracy and the Weimar Republic. The downfall of Brüning is largely the work of Schleicher, who been scheming against him since the beginning of May. Schleicher takes the position of Defense Minister in his friend Papen's government.

June

- June – The Chaco War begins between Bolivia and Paraguay.
- June 4
    - A military coup occurs in Chile.
    - The Papen government dissolves the *Reichstag* for elections on 31 July 1932 in the full expectation that the Nazis will win the largest number of seats.
- June 6 – The Revenue Act of 1932 is enacted, creating the first gas tax in the United States at 1 cent per US gallon (0.26 ¢/L) sold.
- June 14 – The Papen government lifts the ban against the SS and SA in Germany.
- June 16– Lausanne conference opens to discuss reparations, which Germany had not paying since the Hoover Moratorium of June 1931.
- June 20 – The Benelux customs union is negotiated.
- June 24 – After a relatively bloodless military rebellion, Siam becomes a constitutional monarchy.
- June 29 – The comedy serial *Vic and Sade* debuts on NBC Radio.

July

- July 5 – António de Oliveira Salazar becomes the fascist prime minister of Portugal (for the next 36 years).
- July 7 – The French submarine *Prométhée* sinks off Cherbourg; 66 are killed.
- July 8 – The Dow Jones Industrial Average reaches its lowest level of the Great Depression, bottoming out at 41.22.
- July 9
    - The Constitutionalist Revolution starts in Brazil, with the uprising of the state of São Paulo.
    - Lausanne conference ends, agrees to cancel reparations against Germany.
- July 12
    - Norway annexes northern Greenland.

- o Hedley Verity establishes a new first-class cricket record by taking all ten wickets for only ten runs against Nottinghamshire on a pitch affected by a storm.
- July 17 – Altona Bloody Sunday: In Altona, Germany, armed communists attack a National Socialist demonstration; 18 are killed and many other political street fights follow.
- July 20 – The Preußenschlag in Germany. The Papen government sends out the *Reichswehr* under General Gerd von Rundstedt to depose the elected SPD government in Prussia under Otto Braun. The coup gives Papen control of Prussia, the most powerful *Land* in Germany, and is a major blow to German democracy.
- July 21 – British Empire Economic Conference opens in Ottawa, Canada.
- July 28 – U.S. President Herbert Hoover orders the U.S. Army to forcibly evict the Bonus Army of World War I veterans gathered in Washington, D.C. Troops disperse the last of the Bonus Army the next day.
- July 30
  - o The 1932 Summer Olympics open in Los Angeles.
  - o Walt Disney's *Flowers and Trees*, the first animated cartoon to be presented in full Technicolor, premieres in Los Angeles. It releases in theaters, along with the film version of Eugene O'Neill's *Strange Interlude* (starring Norma Shearer and Clark Gable); *Flowers and Trees* goes on to win the first Academy Award for Best Animated Short.
- July 31 – *Reichstag* election sees the Nazis win 37% of the vote, becoming the largest party in the *Reichstag*.

August

- August – A farmers' revolt begins in the Midwestern United States.
- August 1
  - o The second International Polar Year, an international scientific collaboration, begins.
  - o Forrest Mars produces the first Mars bar in his Slough factory in England.

- August 2 – The first positron is discovered by Carl D. Anderson.
- August 5 – Hitler meets with Schleicher and reneges on the "gentlemen's agreement", demanding that he be appointed Chancellor. Schleicher agrees to support Hitler as Chancellor provided that he can remain minister of defense. Schleicher sets up a meeting between Hindenburg and Hitler on for the 13 August to discuss Hitler's possible appointment as chancellor.
- August 6 – The first Venice Film Festival is held.
- August 6 – In Germany the first worldwide Autobahn opened by Konrad Adenauer: Bundesautobahn 555.
- August 6 – Carl Gustaf Ekman resigns as Prime Minister of Sweden, and is replaced by his Minister of Finance Felix Hamrin.
- August 7 – Raymond Edward Welch becomes the first one legged man to scale the 6,288 ft. Mount Washington in New Hampshire.
- August 9 –
  - The Papen government in Germany, which likes to take a tough "law and order" stance, passes via Article 48 a law proscribing the death penalty for a variety of offenses and with the court system simplified so that the courts can hand down as many death sentences as possible.
  - The Potempa Murder case: In the German town of Potempa, five Nazi "Brownshirts" break into the house of Konrad Pietrzuch, a Communist miner, and proceed to castrate and beat him to death in front of his mother. The case attracts much media attention in Germany. The murderers were released from jail after Adolf Hitler became Chancellor of Germany.
- August 10 – A 5.1 kg chondrite-type meteorite breaks fragments and strikes earth near the town of Archie, Missouri.
- August 11 – To celebrate Constitution Day in Germany, Chancellor Franz von Papen and his interior minister Baron Wilhelm von Gayl present proposed amendments to the Weimar constitution for a "New State" to deal with the problems besetting Germany.
- August 13 – Hitler meets President von Hindenburg and asks to be appointed as Chancellor. Hindenburg refuses under the grounds that Hitler is not qualified to be Chancellor and asks him instead to

serve as Vice-Chancellor in Papen's government. Hitler announces his "all or nothing" strategy in which he will oppose any government not headed by himself and will accept no office other than Chancellor.

- August 18 – Auguste Piccard reaches an altitude of 16,197 m (53,140 ft) with a hot air balloon.
- August 18–19 – Scottish aviator Jim Mollison becomes the first pilot to make an East-to-West solo transatlantic flight, from Portmarnock, Dublin, Ireland to Pennfield, New Brunswick, Canada, in his de Havilland Puss Moth biplane *The Heart's Content*.
- August 20 – The Ottawa conference ends with the adoption of Imperial Preference tariff, turning the British Empire into one economic zone with a series of tariffs meant to exclude non-empire states from competing within the markets of Britain; the Dominions; and the rest of the empire.
- August 22 – The five SA men involved in the torture and murder of Konrad Pietrzuch are quickly convicted and sentenced to death under an emergency law introduced by the Papen government on 8 August. The Potempa case becomes a *cause célèbre* in Germany with the Nazis demonstrating for amnesty for the "Potempa five" under the grounds they were justified in killing the Communist Pietrzuch. Hitler sends a telegram congratulating the "Potempa five". Many Germans argue that the "Potempa five" are patriotic heroes who should not be executed while others maintain the death sentences are appropriate given the brutality of the torture and murder.
- August 23 – The Panama Civil Aviation Authority is established.
- August 30 – Hermann Göring is elected as Speaker of the German *Reichstag*.
- August 31 – A total solar eclipse is visible from northern Canada through northeastern Vermont, New Hampshire, southwestern Maine and the Capes of Massachusetts.

September

- September 2 – Despite the court's sentence of death against the "Potempa five", Chancellor von Papen in his capacity as *Reich Commissioner of Prussia* refuses to have the "Potempa five" executed under the grounds that they were not aware of the emergency law at the time they committed the murder, but in reality because he is still hoping for Nazi support for his government.
- September 9 – Generalitat of Catalonia is restored within the Second Spanish Republic from September 25 until the collapse of the Republic in 1939.
- September 9 – Beginning of the Chaco War a conflict between Paraguay and Bolivia because of delimitation problems and others.
- September 10 – The IND Eighth Avenue Line, at this time the world's longest subway line (31 miles (50 km)), begins operation in Manhattan.
- September 11 – Canadian operations end on the International Railway (New York–Ontario).
- September 11 – A bronze statue of Youssef Bey Karam was erected in his memory outside the Cathedral of Saint Georges, Ehden.
- September 12 – The very unpopular Papen government is defeated on a massive motion of no-confidence in the *Reichstag*. With the exceptions of the German People's Party and the German National People's Party, every party in the *Reichstag* votes for the no-confidence motion. Papen has Hindenburg dissolve the *Reichstag* for new elections in November.
- September 20 – Mohandas K. Gandhi begins a hunger strike in Poona prison, India.
- September 22 – Soviet famine of 1932–33 begins, millions starve to death as a result of forced collectivization and as part of the government's effort to break rural resistance to its policies. The Soviet regimes denies the famine and allows millions to die.

- September 23 – The Kingdom of Hejaz and Nejd is proclaimed the Kingdom of Saudi Arabia, concluding the country's unification under the rule of Ibn Saud.
- September 24 – After his party's victory in the election to the Swedish Riksdag's second chamber, Social Democrat Per Albin Hansson becomes the new Prime Minister of Sweden, after Felix Hamrin.
- September 27 – Ryutin Affair at its height in the Soviet Union. The Soviet Politburo meets and condemns the so-called "Ryutin Platform" and agrees to expel those associated with it from the Communist Party, but refuses Stalin's request to execute those associated with the "Ryutin Platform".

October

- October 1 –
    - Babe Ruth makes his famous called shot in the fifth inning of game 3 of the 1932 World Series.
    - Gyula Gömbös becomes Prime Minister of Hungary, the first time a member of the radical right has become Hungary's head of government.
- October 3 – Iraq becomes an independent kingdom under Faisal.
- October 13 – Chief Justice Charles Evans Hughes lays the cornerstone for a new U.S. Supreme Court building.
- October 15
    - Tata Airlines (later to become Air India) makes its first flight.
    - The Michigan Marching Band (at this time called the Varsity band) debuts Script Ohio at the Michigan versus Ohio State game in Columbus.
- October 19 – Prince Gustav Adolf of Sweden marries Princess Sibylla of Saxe-Coburg and Gotha.
- October 23 – Fred Allen's radio comedy show debuts on CBS in the United States.
- October 25 – Twenty-one-year-old Michael D'Oyly Carte, grandson of theatrical impresario and hotelier Richard D'Oyly Carte, is killed in a car crash in Switzerland.

November

The Cipher Bureau breaks the German Enigma cipher and overcomes the ever-growing structural and operating complexities of the evolving Enigma with plugboard, the main German cipher device during World War II.

- November 1 – The San Francisco Opera House opens.
- November 3 – Strike by transport workers in Berlin. The Nazis and the Communists both co-operate in support of the strike. The Nazi-Communist co-operation hurts the Nazis at the upcoming election with many right-wing voters switching back to the German National People's Party.
- November 6 – The *Reichstag* election is held. The Nazis remain the largest party, but their share of the seats drops from 37% to 32%.
- November 7 – *Buck Rogers in the 25th Century* debuts on American radio. It is the first science fiction program on radio.
- November 8 – U.S. presidential election, 1932: Democratic Governor of New York Franklin D. Roosevelt defeats Republican President Herbert Hoover in a landslide victory.
- November 9
  - A hurricane and huge waves kill about 2,500 in Santa Cruz del Sur in the worst natural disaster in Cuban history.
  - Geneva massacre: Military of Switzerland fire on a socialist ant-fascist demonstration in Geneva leaving 13 dead and 60 injured.

- November 16 – New York City's Palace Theatre fully converts to a cinema, which is considered the final death knell of vaudeville as a popular entertainment in the United States.
- November 19 – The second wife of Joseph Stalin is found dead in her home.
- November 21 – German president Hindenburg begins negotiations with Adolf Hitler about the formation of a new government.
- November 24 – In Washington, D.C., the FBI Scientific Crime Detection Laboratory (better known as the FBI Crime Lab) officially opens.
- November 30 – The Polish Cipher Bureau breaks the German Enigma cipher.

December

- December 1 – Germany returns to the World Disarmament Conference after the others powers agree to accept *gleichberechtigung* "in principle". Henceforward, it is clear that Germany will be allowed to rearm beyond the limits imposed by the Treaty of Versailles.
- December 3 – Hindenburg names Kurt von Schleicher as German chancellor after he ousts Papen. Papen is deeply angry about how his former friend Schleicher has brought him down and decides that he will do anything to get back into power.
- December 4 – Chancellor Schleicher meets with Gregor Strasser and offers to appoint him Vice-Chancellor and *Reich* Commissioner for Prussia out of the hope that if faced with a split in the NSDAP, Hitler will support his government.
- December 5 – At a secret meeting of the Nazi leaders, Strasser urges Hitler to drop his "all or nothing" strategy and accept Schleicher's offer to have the Nazis serve in his cabinet. Hitler gives a dramatic speech saying that Schleicher's offer is not acceptable and he will stick to his "all or nothing" strategy whatever the consequences might be and wins the Nazi leadership over to his viewpoint.

- December 8 – Gregor Strasser resigns as the chief of the NSDAP's organizational department in protest against Hitler's "all or nothing" strategy.
- December 12 – Japan and the Soviet Union reform their diplomatic connections.
- December 19 – BBC World Service begins broadcasting as the BBC Empire Service.
- December 23 – A coal mine in Moweaqua, Illinois, kills 54.
- December 24 – A methane gas explosion causes the Moweaqua Coal Mine Disaster which claims 54 lives.
- December 25
    - An earthquake in the Kansu Province in China kills 70,000.
    - IG Farben file a patent application in Germany for the medical application of the first sulfonamide oral antibiotic, which will be marketed as Prontosil, following Gerhard Domagk's laboratory demonstration of its properties as an antibiotic.
- December 27 –
    - *Radio City Music Hall* opens in New York City.
    - Internal passports are introduced in the Soviet Union.
- December 28 – The Cologne banker Kurt von Schröder-who is a close friend of Papen and a NSDAP member-meets with Adolf Hitler to tell him that Papen wants to set up a meeting to discuss how they can work together. Papen wants Nazi support to return to the Chancellorship while Hitler wants Papen to convince Hindenburg to appoint him Chancellor. Hitler agrees to meet Papen on 3 January 1933.

Date unknown

- Dust storms begin in Kansas, Oklahoma, Colorado, New Mexico and Texas, the start of the Dust Bowl in the United States.
- Zippo lighters are developed.
- Zero-length springs are invented, revolutionizing seismometers and gravimeters.

- The Kennedy–Thorndike experiment shows that measured time as well as length are affected by motion, in accordance with the theory of special relativity.
- James Chadwick discovers the neutron.
- Geneticist J. B. S. Haldane publishes *The Causes of Evolution*, unifying the findings of Mendelian genetics with those of evolutionary science.
- The heath hen becomes extinct in North America.
- Walter B. Pitkin publishes *Life Begins at Forty* in the United States.
- The Republican Citizens Committee Against National Prohibition is established for the repeal of Prohibition in the United States.
- Yezd Fire temple (*Atash Behram*) becomes established in Yazd, Iran.
- Association for Research and Enlightenment, Inc. (ARE) founded in Virginia Beach, Virginia, as an open-membership group to research the collected transcripts of Edgar Cayce's continuing trances, stored at the Edgar Cayce Foundation.
- "The Noah of Washington Mud Flats" predicts a Deluge in 1936, building an Ark and demon-proof armor.
- Unemployment in the United States – ca. 33% – 14 million. A similar level of unemployment affects Germany. Many people in depressed countries do not receive unemployment benefit due to governments not being able to afford benefit payments.

Births

January

Umberto Eco

Piper Laurie

- January 1 – Tzaims Luksus, American artist and fashion designer
- January 2 – Jean Little, Canadian author
- January 3 – Dabney Coleman, American actor
- January 5
    - Johnny Adams, American singer (d. 1998)
    - Umberto Eco, Italian scholar and novelist (d. 2016)
- January 6 – Stuart A. Rice, American chemist
- January 11 – Takkō Ishimori, Japanese voice actor (d. 2013)
- January 13 – Joseph Cardinal Zen, Catholic Bishop of Hong Kong
- January 15 – Cleven "Goodie" Goudeau, American art director and cartoonist (d. 2015)
- January 16 – Dian Fossey, American zoologist (d. 1985)
- January 17 – Sheree North, American actress and singer (d. 2005)
- January 18 – Robert Anton Wilson, American author (d. 2007)
- January 22 – Piper Laurie, American actress
- January 23
    - George Allen, English footballer
    - Jack Gilbert Graham, American mass murderer (d. 1957)
- January 25 – Nikolay Anikin, Soviet cross-country skier (d. 2009)
- January 26 – Coxsone Dodd, Jamaican record producer (d. 2004)
- January 28 – Don McMichael, Australian public servant
- January 29 – Tommy Taylor, English footballer (d. 1958)
- January 30
    - Kazuo Inamori, Japanese businessman
    - Knock Yokoyama, Japanese comedian and politician (d. 2007)

February

John Williams

Edward Kennedy

Johnny Cash

Elizabeth Taylor

- February 1
  - John Nott, British politician
  - Hassan Al-Turabi, Sudanese spiritual leader (d. 2016)
- February 3 – Peggy Ann Garner, American actress (d. 1984)
- February 5 – Cesare Maldini, Italian football player and manager (d. 2016)
- February 6 – François Truffaut, French film director (d. 1984)
- February 7 – Gay Talese, American author
- February 8
  - Jean Saunders, English writer (d. 2011)
  - John Williams, American composer and conductor
- February 9 – Gerhard Richter, German painter
- February 11
  - Margit Carlqvist, Swedish actress
  - Jerome Lowenthal, American pianist
  - Dennis Skinner, British politician
- February 12 – Julian Lincoln Simon, American economist and author (d. 1998)
- February 13 – Susan Oliver, American actress (d. 1990)
- February 14 – Alexander Kluge, German author and film director
- February 16
  - Harry Goz, American actor (d. 2003)
  - Alhaji Ahmad Tejan Kabbah, former President of Sierra Leone (d. 2014)
  - Antonio Ordóñez, Spanish bullfighter (d. 1998)
  - Gretchen Wyler, American dancer, actress and animal rights activist (d. 2007)
- February 18 – Miloš Forman, Czech film director
- February 20 – Adrian Cristobal, Filipino writer (d. 2007)
- February 22
  - Edward Kennedy, American politician (d. 2009)
  - Robert Opron, French automotive designer
- February 23
  - Majel Barrett, American actress (d. 2008)
  - Bill Bonds, American former television newscaster (d. 2014)
- February 24 – Michel Legrand, French composer
- February 25 – Faron Young, American country singer (d. 1996)

- February 26 – Johnny Cash, American country singer (d. 2003)
- February 27 – Dame Elizabeth Taylor, British-American actress (d. 2011)
- February 28 – Don Francks, Canadian actor (d. 2016)

March

John Updike

- March – Dennis O'Neill, young victim of manslaughter by foster parents (d. 1945)
- March 4
  - Ryszard Kapuściński, Polish journalist (d. 2007)
  - Miriam Makeba, South African singer (d. 2008)
  - Ed Roth, American car designer (d. 2001)
  - Frank Wells, American entertainment businessman (d. 1994)
- March 6 – Bronisław Geremek, Polish social historian and politician (d. 2008)
- March 7 – Momoko Kōchi, Japanese actress (d. 1998)
- March 12 – Andrew Young, U.S. Ambassador to the United Nations
- March 14 – Mark Murphy, American jazz singer (d. 2015)
- March 16 – Don Blasingame, Major League Baseball player and Japanese baseball manager (d. 2005)
- March 17 – Donald N. Langenberg, American physicist
- March 18 – John Updike, American author (d. 2009)
- March 21 – Walter Gilbert, American chemist, Nobel Prize laureate
- March 22 – Els Borst, Dutch politician, Deputy Prime Minister of the Netherlands (1998-2002) (d. 2014)
- March 30 – Ted Morgan, French-born biographer and journalist
- March 31 – Nagisa Oshima, Japanese film director (d. 2013)

April

Debbie Reynolds

Omar Sharif

Tiny Tim

- April 1
  - Gordon Jump, American actor (d. 2003)
  - Debbie Reynolds, American actress, singer and dancer

- April 2
  - Michael Vernon, Australian consumer activist (d. 1993)
  - Edward Egan, American cardinal (d. 2015)
- April 4
  - Anthony Perkins, American actor (d. 1992)
  - Andrei Tarkovsky, Russian film director (d. 1986)
- April 8 – Sultan Iskandar of Johor, also the 8th Yang di-Pertuan Agong of Malaysia (d. 2010)
- April 9
  - Armin Jordan, Swiss conductor (d. 2006)
  - Carl Perkins, American musician (d. 1998)
- April 10
  - Omar Sharif, Egyptian actor (d. 2015)
  - Blaze Starr, American burlesque artist (d. 2015)
- April 11 – Joel Grey, American actor, singer and dancer
- April 12
  - Lakshman Kadirgamar, Sri Lankan politician (d. 2005)
  - Tiny Tim, American musician (d. 1996)
- April 14 – Loretta Lynn, American country singer
- April 21 – Elaine May, American movie director
- April 23 – Halston, American fashion designer (d. 1990)
- April 25 – William Roache, English actor
- April 26 – Michael Smith, English-born chemist, Nobel Prize laureate (d. 2000)
- April 27
  - Casey Kasem, American disc jockey and voice actor (d. 2014)
  - Gian-Carlo Rota, Italian-born mathematician and philosopher (d. 1999)
  - Anouk Aimée, French actress
- April 28 – Brownie Ledbetter, American civil rights activist (d. 2010)

May

- May 6 – Ahmet Haxhiu, Albanian political activist (d. 1994)
- May 7

- o Jordi Bonet, Canadian artist (d. 1979)
- o Jenny Joseph, English poet
- May 8
  - o Phyllida Law, Scottish actress
  - o Sonny Liston, American boxer (d. 1970)
- May 9 – Geraldine McEwan, Scottish actress (d. 2015)
- May 11 – Valentino, Italian fashion designer
- May 17 – Chris Ballingall, American baseball player
- May 19 – Alma Cogan, English singer (d. 1966)
- May 21 – Leonidas Vasilikopoulos, Greek admiral and intelligence chief (d. 2014)
- May 24 – Arnold Wesker, British playwright (d. 2016)
- May 25
  - o Roger Bowen, American actor (d. 1996)
  - o John Gregory Dunne, American writer (d. 2003)
  - o K. C. Jones, American basketball player and coach
- May 29 – Paul R. Ehrlich, American biologist

June

Pat Morita

- June 4
  - o John Drew Barrymore, American actor (d. 2004)
  - o Maurice Shadbolt, New Zealand writer (d. 2004)
- June 9 – Jack Imel, American singer
- June 12 – Rona Jaffe, American novelist (d. 2005)
- June 13 – Rainer K. Sachs, German-American physicist and biologist
- June 15 – Mario Cuomo, American politician (d. 2015)
- June 18

- o Dudley R. Herschbach, American chemist, Nobel Prize laureate
- o Geoffrey Hill, English poet
- June 19 – José Sanchis Grau, Spanish comic writer (d. 2011)
- June 21 – O. C. Smith American musician (d. 2001)
- June 22
  - o Soraya Esfandiary-Bakhtiari, princess of Iran, Queen Consort of Mohammad Reza Pahlavi (d. 2001)
  - o Prunella Scales, English actress
- June 25 – Peter Blake, English artist
- June 27 – Anna Moffo, American operatic soprano (d. 2006)
- June 28 – Pat Morita, Asian-American actor (d. 2005)

July

Donald Rumsfeld

- July 2
  - o Waldemar Matuška, Czech singer (d. 2009)
  - o Dave Thomas, American fast-food entrepreneur (d. 2002)
- July 4 – Otis Young, African-American actor (d. 2001)
- July 5 – Gyula Horn, Prime Minister of Hungary (d. 2013)
- July 7 – Eileen Lemass, Irish politician
- July 8 – John Pascal, American playwright, screenwriter, author, and journalist (d. 1981)
- July 9 – Donald Rumsfeld, former U.S. Secretary of Defense
- July 12 – Otis Davis, American runner
- July 13 – Per Nørgård, Danish composer
- July 16
  - o Tim Asch, Anthropologist, photographer and ethnographic filmmaker (d. 1994)
  - o Max McGee, American football player (d. 2007)

- July 17 – Yukio Aoshima, Japanese politician and comedian (d. 2006)
- July 20
  - Dick Giordano, American comic book artist and editor (d. 2010)
  - Ove Verner Hansen, Danish actor
  - Nam June Paik, Korean-born American artist (d. 2006)
  - Otto Schily, German politician
- July 21
  - Norman Geisler, American Christian author, theologian, and philosopher
  - Ernie Warlick, American football player (d. 2012)
- July 29 – Nancy Landon Kassebaum Baker, U.S. Senator
- July 31 – John Searle, American philosopher

August

Peter O'Toole

Abebe Bikila

Banharn Silpa-archa

- August 1
  - Meir Kahane, American-born Israeli rabbi and ultra-nationalist figure (d. 1990)
  - Meena Kumari, Indian actress (d. 1972)
- August 2
  - Lamar Hunt, American sportsman (d. 2006)
  - Peter O'Toole, British-Irish actor (d. 2013)
- August 6 – Howard Hodgkin, British painter and print-maker
- August 7
  - Abebe Bikila, Ethiopian long-distance runner (d. 1973)
  - Maurice Rabb, Jr., African-American ophthalmologist (d. 2005)
- August 8 – Mel Tillis, American country singer
- August 11 – Fernando Arrabal, Spanish writer
- August 12
  - Charlie O'Donnell, American game show announcer (d. 2010)
  - Sirikit, Queen of Thailand (from 1950 to present)
- August 15
  - Abby Dalton, American actress
  - Jim Lange, American disc jockey and game show host (d. 2014)
- August 17 – V. S. Naipaul, West Indian-born writer, Nobel Prize laureate
- August 18 – William R. Bennett, Premier of British Columbia (d. 2015)

- August 19 – Banharn Silpa-archa, 32nd Prime Minister of Thailand (d. 2016)
- August 20 – Vasily Aksyonov, Russian writer (d. 2009)
- August 24 – W. Morgan Sheppard, British actor
- August 25 – Luis Félix López, Ecuadorian writer and politician (d. 2008)
- August 27 – Mohamed Hamri, Moroccan artist (d. 2000)

September

Algirdas Brazauskas

Adolfo Suárez

Manmohan Singh

- September 1
  - Sunny von Bülow, American socialite (d. 2008)
  - Derog Gioura, Nauruan politician and former President of Nauru (d. 2008)
- September 3 – Eileen Brennan, American actress and singer (d. 2013)
- September 4 – Dinsdale Landen, British actor (d. 2003)
- September 5 – Carol Lawrence, American actress, singer and dancer
- September 6 – Marguerite Pearson, American professional baseball player (d. 2005)
- September 7 – John Paul Getty, Jr., American-born philanthropist (d. 2003)
- September 8 – Patsy Cline, American singer (d. 1963)
- September 11 – Peter Anderson, English footballer
- September 13 – Fernando González Pacheco, Colombian television host, announcer, journalist and actor (d. 2014)
- September 18 – Nikolay Rukavishnikov, Russian cosmonaut (d. 2002)
- September 21 – Mickey Kuhn, American child actor
- September 22 – Algirdas Brazauskas, President of Lithuania (d. 2010)
- September 25
  - Glenn Gould, Canadian pianist (d. 1982)
  - Charles Stanley, American televangelist
  - Adolfo Suárez, 1st Spanish Prime Minister after the dictatorship of Franco (d. 2014)
- September 26
  - Donna Douglas, American actress (*The Beverly Hillbillies*) (d. 2015)
  - Richard Herd, American actor
  - Joyce Jameson, American actress (d. 1987)
  - Manmohan Singh, Prime Minister of India
- September 27 – Oliver E. Williamson, American economist
- September 28 – Víctor Jara, Chilean singer-songwriter (d. 1973)
- September 29 – Mehmood, Indian actor (d. 2004)
- September 30 – Shintarō Ishihara, Japanese author and politician

October

- October 3 – Hugh Curtis, Canadian politician (d. 2014)
- October 4 – Milan Chvostek, Canadian television director
- October 5 – Michael John Rogers, English ornithologist (d. 2006)
- October 8 – Ray Reardon, Welsh snooker player
- October 9 – David Plowden, American photographer
- October 10 – Harry Smith, English footballer
- October 11 – Dottie West, American singer/songwriter (d. 1991)
- October 12
  - Dick Gregory, American comedian and activist
  - Yuichiro Miura, Japanese alpinist
  - Ned Jarrett, American racing driver and broadcaster
- October 13 – Jean Edward Smith, American political scientist and biographer
- October 14 – Wolf Vostell, German artist (d. 1998)
- October 18 – Vytautas Landsbergis, Lithuanian politician
- October 19 – Robert Reed, American actor (d. 1992)
- October 20
  - Rosey Brown, American football player (d. 2004)
  - William Christopher, American actor
  - Rokurō Naya, Japanese voice actor, younger brother of the late Gorō Naya (d. 2014)
- October 24
  - Pierre-Gilles de Gennes, French physicist, Nobel Prize laureate (d. 2007)
  - Robert Mundell, Canadian economist, Nobel Prize laureate
- October 27
  - Harry Gregg, Northern Irish footballer and football manager
  - Dolores Moore, American baseball player (d. 2000)
  - Sylvia Plath, American poet and author (d. 1963)
- October 28
  - Spyros Kyprianou, President of Cyprus (d. 2002)
  - Suzy Parker, American fashion model and actress (d. 2003)
- October 31 – Iemasa Kayumi, Japanese voice actor, actor and narrator (d. 2014)

November

Roy Scheider

Jacques Chirac

- November 3 – Albert Reynolds, eighth Taoiseach of Ireland (d. 2014)
- November 4
    - Thomas Klestil, President of Austria (d. 2004)
    - Noam Pitlik, American actor and director (d. 1999)
- November 10
    - Paul Bley, Canadian pianist (d. 2016)
    - Don Henderson, British actor (d. 1997)
    - Roy Scheider, American actor (d. 2008)
- November 11 – Germano Mosconi, Italian journalist (d. 2012)
- November 12 – Jerry Douglas, American actor
- November 13 – Richard Mulligan, American actor (d. 2000)
- November 15
    - Petula Clark, British singer, actress, and songwriter
    - Clyde McPhatter, American singer (d. 1972)
- November 18 – Yoyoy Villame, Filipino singer and actor (d. 2007)
- November 20 – Richard Dawson, British-born comedian and game show host (d. 2012)
- November 21 – Pelle Gudmundsen-Holmgreen, Danish composer

- November 22
  - Robert Vaughn, American actor
  - Keith Wickenden, British politician (d. 1983)
- November 27 – Benigno Aquino, Jr., Filipino politician and senator (d. 1983)
- November 29 – Jacques Chirac, President of France

December

Corry Brokken

- December 1 – Dame Heather Begg, New Zealand mezzo-soprano (d. 2009)
- December 2 – Sergio Bonelli, Italian comic book author and publisher (d. 2011)
- December 3 – Corry Brokken, Dutch singer, Eurovision Song Contest 1957 winner (d. 2016)
- December 4 – Roh Tae-woo, President of South Korea
- December 5
  - Sheldon Lee Glashow, American physicist
  - Little Richard, American singer and evangelist
- December 7
  - Paul Caponigro, American photographer
  - Rosemary Rogers, Sri Lankan-born American novelist
  - J. B. Sumarlin, Indonesian economist and a former Minister of Finance
- December 9
  - Morton Downey, Jr., American television personality (d. 2001)
  - Bill Hartack, American jockey (d. 2007)
- December 11 – Enrique Bermúdez, Nicaraguan Contra leader (d. 1991)
- December 13 – Tatsuya Nakadai, Japanese actor

- December 17 – Kelly E. Taggart, American admiral and civil engineer, second Director of the National Oceanic and Atmospheric Administration Commissioned Officer Corps (d. 2014)
- December 21 – Edward Hoagland, American essayist
- December 24 – Earl Dodge, American temperance movement leader (d. 2007)
- December 28
    - Dhirubhai Ambani, Indian businessman (d. 2002)
    - Dorsey Burnette, American singer (d. 1979)
    - Roy Hattersley, Baron Hattersley, British politician and life peer
    - Nichelle Nichols, American actress and singer
    - Manuel Puig, Argentinian writer (d. 1990)
    - Titien Sumarni, Indonesian actress (d. 1966)
- December 29 – Inga Swenson, American actress and singer
- December 31 – Felix Rexhausen, German journalist, editor and author (d. 1992)

Date unknown

- Basil Blackshaw, Northern Irish artist
- Irene Jai Narayan, Fiji politician (d. 2011)

Deaths

January

Paul Doumer

- January 2 – Paul Pau, French general (b. 1848)
- January 7 – André Maginot, French soldier and politician (b. 1877)

- January 8 – Eurosia Fabris, Italian Catholic *Blessed* (b. 1866)
- January 13– Ernest Mangnall, English football manager (b. 1866)
- January 21 – Lytton Strachey, British writer and biographer (b. 1880)
- January 24 – Sir Alfred Yarrow, English shipbuilder and philanthropist (b. 1842)
- January 26 – William Wrigley, Jr., American chewing gum industrialist (b. 1861)

February

Edgar Wallace

- February 1 – Farabundo Martí, Salvadorean revolutionary (murdered) (b. 1893)
- February 8 – Yordan Milanov, Bulgarian architect (b. 1867)
- February 8 – Mad Dog Coll, American gangster (b. 1908)
- February 10 – Edgar Wallace, English novelist and screenwriter (b. 1875)
- February 15 – Minnie Maddern Fiske, American actress (b. 1865)
- February 16 – Ferdinand Buisson, French pacifist, recipient of the Nobel Peace Prize (b. 1841)
- February 17 – Albert Johnson, Canadian criminal (b. ?)
- February 18 – Frederick Augustus III, last King of Saxony (b. 1865)
- February 29 – Ramon Casas i Carbó, Spanish painter (b. 1866)

March

- March 1
  - Frank Teschemacher, American musician (b. 1906)
  - Dino Campana, Italian poet (b. 1885)
- March 4 – Fawcet Wray, British admiral (b. 1873)
- March 6 – John Philip Sousa, American band leader, conductor, and composer (*The Stars and Stripes Forever*) (b. 1854)
- March 7
  - Heinrich Clam-Martinic, Austrian statesman, former Prime Minister (b. 1863)
  - Aristide Briand, French statesman, recipient of the Nobel Peace Prize (b. 1862)
- March 11 – Dora Carrington, British painter (b. 1893)
- March 10 – Paolo Boselli, 22nd Prime Minister of Italy (b. 1838)
- March 17 – Iliaz Vrioni, Albanian statesman, former Prime Minister (b. 1882)
- March 14 – George Eastman, American inventor (*Kodak*) (b. 1854)
- March 18 – Chauncey Olcott, American stage actor and singer-songwriter (b. 1858)
- March 31 – Eben Byers, American steel tycoon and socialite (radiation poisoning) (b. 1880)

April

Wilhelm Ostwald

- April 2
  - Rose Coghlan, English actress (b. 1851)

- o Bill Pickett, African-American cowboy whose parents were slaves (b. 1870)
- April 4 – Wilhelm Ostwald, German chemist, Nobel Prize laureate (b. 1853)
- April 7 – Grigore Constantinescu, Romanian priest and journalist (b. 1875)
- April 20 – Giuseppe Peano, Italian mathematician (b. 1858)
- April 22 – Ferenc Oslay, Hungarian-Slovene historian, writer and irredenta (b. 1883)
- April 26 – William Lockwood, English cricketer (b. 1868)
- April 27 – Hart Crane, American poet (b. 1899)
- April 29 – José Félix Uriburu, 22nd President of Argentina (b. 1868)

May

- May 3
  - o Henri de Gaulle, father of Charles de Gaulle (b. 1848)
  - o Charles Fort, American researcher of the unusual (b. 1874)
- May 7 – Paul Doumer, President of France (assassinated) (b. 1857)
- May 15 – Tsuyoshi Inukai, Prime Minister of Japan (assassinated) (b. 1855)
- May 17 – Frederick C. Billard, Commandant of the United States Coast Guard (b. 1873)
- May 22 – Augusta, Lady Gregory, Irish writer and folklorist (b. 1852)
- May 25 – Franz von Hipper, German admiral (b. 1863)
- May 30 – John Hubbard, American admiral (b. 1849)

June

- June 3 – Dorabji Tata, Indian businessman (b. 1859)
- June 13 – Alexander Bethell, British admiral (b. 1855)
- June 16 – Felipe Segundo Guzmán, 35th President of Bolivia (b. 1879)
- June 21 – Major Taylor, American cyclist (b. 1878)
- June 24 – Ernst Põdder, Estonian military commander (b. 1879)

- June 27 – Francis P. Duffy, Canadian American Roman Catholic priest (b. 1871)
- June 29 – William Humble Ward, 2nd Earl of Dudley, 4th Governor-General of Australia (b. 1867)

July

- July 2 – Manuel II of Portugal, last king of Portugal (b. 1889)
- July 6 – Kenneth Grahame, Scottish-born author (*The Wind In The Willows*) (b. 1859)
- July 7 – Henry Eyster Jacobs, American Lutheran theologian (b. 1844)
- July 16 – Herbert Plumer, 1st Viscount Plumer, British general (b. 1857)
- July 22
  - Errico Malatesta, Italian anarchist (b. 1853)
  - Florenz Ziegfeld, Broadway impresario (b. 1867)
- July 23
  - Tenby Davies, Welsh half-mile world champion runner (b. 1884)
  - Alberto Santos-Dumont, Brazilian aviation pioneer (suicide) (b. 1873)
- July 27 – Archduchess Gisela of Austria (b. 1856)

August

Kate M. Gordon

- August 2
  - Dan Brouthers, American baseball player and MLB Hall of Famer (b. 1858)
  - Ignaz Seipel, two-time Chancellor of Austria (b. 1876)
- August 19 – Johann Schober, three-time Chancellor of Austria (b. 1874)
- August 24 – Kate M. Gordon, American suffragette (b. 1861)

September

- September 5 – Paul Bern, American screenwriter (b. 1889)
- September 8 – Christian von Ehrenfels, Austrian philosopher (b. 1859)
- September 16 – Ronald Ross, English physician, recipient of the Nobel Prize in Physiology or Medicine (b. 1857)
- September 18 – Peg Entwistle, film actress (b. 1908)
- September 20 – Wovoka, Paiute visionary (*Ghost Dance*) (b. c. 1856)
- September 23 – Jules Chéret, French poster designer (b. 1836)
- September 25 – Joel R. P. Pringle, American admiral (b. 1873)

October

- October 5 – Christopher Brennan, Australian poet and scholar (b. 1870)
- October 17 – Lucy Bacon, American painter (b. 1857)
- October 26 – Molly Brown, Denver socialite, noted survivor of the sinking of the RMS *Titanic* (b. 1867)
- October 30 – Paul Methuen, 3rd Baron Methuen, British field marshal (b. 1845)

November

- November 4 – Belle Bennett, American actress (b. 1891)
- November 15 – Charles Waddell Chesnutt, African American author, essayist and political activist (b. 1858)
- November 22 – William Walker Atkinson, American writer (b. 1862)

December

- December 2 – Amadeo Vives, Spanish composer (b. 1871)
- December 4 – Gustav Meyrink, Austrian writer (b. 1868)
- December 8 – Gertrude Jekyll, English garden designer, writer and artist (b. 1843)
- December 9
  - Roquia Sakhawat Hussain, Bangladeshi writer and social worker (b. 1880)
  - Isa ibn Ali Al Khalifa, Hakim of Bahrain (b. 1848)
- December 18 – Eduard Bernstein, German socialist (b. 1850)
- December 19 – Yun Bong-gil, Korean resister against Japanese occupation of Korea (b. 1908; executed)
- December 28 – Malcolm Whitman, American tennis player (b. 1877)

Date unknown

- Vittorio Alinari, Italian photographer (b. 1859)

Nobel Prizes

- Physics – Werner Karl Heisenberg
- Chemistry – Irving Langmuir
- Physiology or Medicine – Sir Charles Scott Sherrington, Edgar Douglas Adrian
- Literature – John Galsworthy
- Peace – not awarded

In the News

Al Capone convicted for Income Tax Evasion.

The Tenth Summer Olympic Games Opens in Los Angeles.

Amelia Earhart becomes the first woman to make a solo air crossing of the Atlantic Ocean.

The Parking meter is invented in Oklahoma.

Charles Lindbergh son is kidnapped.

Sydney Harbor Bridge Opens on March 19th.

United States Great Depression.

The Winter Olympic Games are held in Lake Placid, New York, United States.

1932 Calendar

January 1932

Sun	Mon	Tue	Wed	Thu	Fri	Sat
					1	2
3	4	5	6	7	8	9
10	11	12	13	14	15	16
17	18	19	20	21	22	23
24	25	26	27	28	29	30
31						

February 1932

Sun	Mon	Tue	Wed	Thu	Fri	Sat
	1	2	3	4	5	6
7	8	9	10	11	12	13
14	15	16	17	18	19	20
21	22	23	24	25	26	27
28	29					

March 1932

Sun	Mon	Tue	Wed	Thu	Fri	Sat
		1	2	3	4	5
6	7	8	9	10	11	12
13	14	15	16	17	18	19
20	21	22	23	24	25	26
27	28	29	30	31		

April 1932

Sun	Mon	Tue	Wed	Thu	Fri	Sat
					1	2
3	4	5	6	7	8	9
10	11	12	13	14	15	16
17	18	19	20	21	22	23
24	25	26	27	28	29	30

May 1932

Sun	Mon	Tue	Wed	Thu	Fri	Sat
1	2	3	4	5	6	7
8	9	10	11	12	13	14
15	16	17	18	19	20	21
22	23	24	25	26	27	28
29	30	31				

June 1932

Sun	Mon	Tue	Wed	Thu	Fri	Sat
			1	2	3	4
5	6	7	8	9	10	11
12	13	14	15	16	17	18
19	20	21	22	23	24	25
26	27	28	29	30		

July 1932

Sun	Mon	Tue	Wed	Thu	Fri	Sat
					1	2
3	4	5	6	7	8	9
10	11	12	13	14	15	16
17	18	19	20	21	22	23
24	25	26	27	28	29	30
31						

August 1932

Sun	Mon	Tue	Wed	Thu	Fri	Sat
	1	2	3	4	5	6
7	8	9	10	11	12	13
14	15	16	17	18	19	20
21	22	23	24	25	26	27
28	29	30	31			

September 1932

Sun	Mon	Tue	Wed	Thu	Fri	Sat
				1	2	3
4	5	6	7	8	9	10
11	12	13	14	15	16	17
18	19	20	21	22	23	24
25	26	27	28	29	30	

October 1932

Sun	Mon	Tue	Wed	Thu	Fri	Sat
						1
2	3	4	5	6	7	8
9	10	11	12	13	14	15
16	17	18	19	20	21	22
23	24	25	26	27	28	29
30	31					

November 1932

Sun	Mon	Tue	Wed	Thu	Fri	Sat
		1	2	3	4	5
6	7	8	9	10	11	12
13	14	15	16	17	18	19
20	21	22	23	24	25	26
27	28	29	30			

December 1932

Sun	Mon	Tue	Wed	Thu	Fri	Sat
				1	2	3
4	5	6	7	8	9	10
11	12	13	14	15	16	17
18	19	20	21	22	23	24
25	26	27	28	29	30	31

Printed in Great Britain
by Amazon

76314636R00031